To Raya With Love

16 Inspired Lessons
For The Young Adult in You

Windi Floyd Reynolds

1

WOM
ENTERPRISES

www.womenterprises.com

Contact Author:
Windi Floyd Reynolds
www.focusedink.com
focusedink@gmail.com

F-ink-CUSED

Website Design:
Reynolds Group Services LLC
Michael Reynolds
reynoldsgroups@gmail.com

Preface

This book was written from a place of love. Grown from inspiration simply in a name, Toraya Jai Garvin.

This little girl, this young adult, Toraya who died at the age of 16 after a battle with Leukemia, had an effect on me and so many. She was kind, she was selfless, and she was caring. She had big dreams and wanted to soar. Her impact was endless. She has caused so many to change how they treat others and how they view life. She showed in her life and her death that being weak does not mean you are not strong. Although she was weak physically due to the cancer, her spirit remained strong. The spirit of Toraya ignited a power within me to complete a goal of my own.

For years, one of my major goals in life was to write a book. I would start and never finish. I even have floppy disks and Yahoo emails as proof of my constant battles of the undone.

I was, and still am my own biggest critic, self-doubt would always overtake me. However, my self-doubt began to become smothered by all the inspiration and greatness around me and what grew inside of me instead was motivation.

Author Cheryl Polote-Williamson once said, "Stop setting goals without an end date."

I was inspired.

I begin to think how my mother in-law Denise Polote-Kelly (also an author) who experienced loss not the same as my own, but a loss and greatness grew from it.

Again, I was inspired.

As I reflect on past inspirations that were all around me as self-doubt festered in my soul, I smile at its greatness. When I arrived at Savannah State University, one of the first people I met was Professor Kai Walker who would later become my college mentor. Kai, a Mass Communication professor at SSU who graduated from Savannah College of Art and Design, mirrored the image of who I could become professionally.

Mentally Inspired.

Thinking back at the start of it all, remembering how my own mother Jannie, who worked two jobs to take care of us, five kids, she too has been inspiring me since a very young age. Inspiration at its finest to know first-hand with hard work; single or married a woman could do all things. Inspiration can be drawn from a variety of places. When your inspiration comes from a place of love or even heartache, the results can be amazing.

Looking back, I was approaching my destiny all wrong, and with all the inspiration surrounding me, the birth of this book, To Raya with Love was created.

This book is a guide for the young adult or the young adult in you which can be someone older in age still navigating their way through life; going through the typical life situations and struggles that most of us do.

These 16 inspired lessons, the number of lessons representative of the number of years Toraya graced this earth are to be used as a guide through your life journey. Some lessons are short, and to the point, and others a little more detailed are tokens of wisdom that I have picked up along the way, learning from my journey and the journey of others.

Use this book to journal your life lessons. Before each lesson you will be asked a question. Fill in your answer. Read the lesson and use the journal pages after each lesson to document and to explore your personal journey. Ultimately, your life lessons can be used to inspire and/or to reignite a fire within.

The lessons are my personal life experiences that I have been inspired to share because I am no longer afraid to live my life to its fullest potential, thanks to Raya.

Table of Contents

Toraya you are the inspiration.

In one sentence who inspires you?

_____

_____

_____

Life Lesson 1
Be Inspired, Become an Inspiration

Inspiration can be and stem from so many things. Inspiration can be beautiful. Inspiration can be sad. Inspiration can be anger. There will be people, things, and moments that happen in your life that cause you to reflect and look at life in a way that you never have before.

When moments or people have an effect on you to the point where you step back and begin to reevaluate yourself, inspiration is happening. Your reevaluation of self may be one where you ask if there is something about myself that I need to change, to improve upon, to remove from my life or to even add to my life.

Someone in your life may inspire you to achieve a goal you never thought you could, a beautiful inspiration.

You may lose someone in your life that changes the course in the way you live your life, an inspiration that is rooted in sadness but evokes a joyful reaction. You may experience or be a witness to an injustice and be inspired to stand up for the rights of those who are too weak or unable to stand, an inspiration that stems from anger and causes an impulsive response.

When the actions of others cause you to act, act up! Act up not in the sense of "acting up or to misbehave," but act up and reach for the sky. Let your actions go beyond your wildest dreams or personal expectations. Act up beyond what others perceive you to be. Act up and out of the norm so that those following you will look up in amazement at what you have done. The same way your inspirations (person, place or thing) have inspired you, you yourself can be an inspiration to others.

My Ultimate Inspiration

There have been quite a few individuals in my life that have inspired me. However, it wasn't until we lost Toraya that I was inspired to jump out there and be great beyond my wildest dreams. I was inspired to complete some of the goals that I have been letting mildew in the back of my mind for years. Toraya caused me to look at life differently.

She caused me to know and believe that life is short. 'Truly short.' The loss of a child is one that is so hard to grasp that you really begin to understand that life is truly out of our control. Clearly, there is a higher power in order. Don't get me wrong, I never thought I truly had control of everything that takes place in my life, but Toraya's death confirmed it for me.

The entire experience was one where I just knew everything was okay and unbeknownst to me it was not okay and things would never be the same afterward for me and so many others.

So, I took my sadness, and I was inspired. I was inspired by a little girl who I had been hearing stories day to day about while working with her mother for over 10 years. I lived for the "Ray Ray" (as we so affectionately called her) moments. I was always excited for her wins and sad for her losses as if she was my own child for years before I had even given birth to my own son, Micah.

I felt I was so connected that I was inspired many years ago to gauge my career goals around her graduation from high school. I said to myself and my co-workers back then, "I will not still be working here when 'Ray Ray' graduates from high school." I smile at that goal because the longer I was a co-worker of her mother, the more the inspiration of 'Ray Ray' poured into me.

I was inspired by the fact that no matter how much you plan, you don't know where life will take you. You are on a ride. You ride that ride until your time is up. However, still up for debate by many on where you head after the ride is over. I know where Toraya is now, so innocent, I can only hope to be there one day.

Your Journal Entry of Inspiration:

What are some examples of people who have inspired you?

How can you use the inspiration you have experienced as motivation for something life changing?

_____

_____

_____

_____

_____

_____

_____

_____

_____

_____

_____

Toraya tried her best at everything she loved.

**Do you believe that we are
all imperfect humans?**

Yes or No?

_____

_____

_____

Share and Be an Inspiration
Post who inspires you with the hashtag
#torayawithlove

FB:
https://facebook.com/groups/torayawithlove

IG:
@focusedink

or submit via Author's site
www.focusedink.com/reviews

Life Lesson 2
Imperfection is Perfection

Perfection is an unattainable goal by nature. However, throughout the journey of your life, you may find yourself in a constant need to be perfect. Your family, your peers, and society may place levels of perfection on you when it comes to your knowledge, your abilities, your appearance, your social status, and the list can go on. How you discern between what you should listen and leave versus what you should listen and take with you makes all the difference.

You will notice that those that place these expectations on you, they themselves find the same or similar expectations hard to reach personally but it does not necessarily mean that you shouldn't take their expectations into consideration. You will come across people in life who want for you what they could never be. Most times your parents are the people in your life that appear to want perfection. You may try hard and find it difficult to reach the levels of perfections being asked of you. You may also wonder how your parents tell you one thing but show you another. Note that most times parents have walked in similar shoes as yours.

The shoes they wore may now have become torn, dirty, and worn out. It's in part because they have gone through the struggles that life can present and in turn they want you to avoid the mistakes they have made. They want a million times more for you than you may want for yourself. So, they may ask of you things that they don't necessarily ask of themselves because they put you on a level higher than they

20

place themselves. So, as you walk through life, know that perfection is impossible but realizing how to be the best version of you is priceless. Once you learn how to be the best version of you and continue to improve each day on who you are, then your imperfections will become perfected in time.

An Imperfection of My Own

I am so imperfect. We all are. I over think, I overanalyze my wrongs and imperfections. Personally, I never set a goal of doing most of the things I have accomplished in life. The only goal I could ever remember putting out there in the universe was to become a writer. However, I never felt good enough, and I didn't know anyone who had accomplished that goal personally. So, even though I knew there were tons of writers in the world, I still could never think to include myself as one professionally.

Nevertheless, if I look back at where I was and if I was to actually believe in myself back then, WOW, the sky would have been the limit. If I had really taken the time and invested in me from a teenager; who knows where I would be now. Life took me on a journey of twists and turns. These twists and turns still lead me to where I am now, and I am thankful, but I had to learn as the years passed that I had to set goals and complete them.

I had to begin to look at myself as having potential beyond measure. I had to allow myself to be vulnerable and to get to know me and improve upon who I was on a daily basis. Once I begin the journey of getting to know myself, my imperfections did not seem so imperfect. I was just me.

Your Journal Entry of Inspiration:
What are some of your imperfections?

_____

_____

_____

_____

_____

_____

_____

_____

_____

_____

_____

_____

_____

_____

_____

Toraya always took Self into Consideration.

In your life who normally comes first yourself or others? Choose one.

_____

_____

_____

Share and Be an Inspiration
Post who inspires you with the hashtag
#torayawithlove

FB:
https://facebook.com/groups/torayawithlove

IG:
@focusedink

or submit via Author's site
www.focusedink.com/reviews

25

Life Lesson 3
Consider Yourself

Taking self into consideration first is not a bad thing. If you don't take care of yourself, then you can be of no help or value to anyone else. To be selfless is great but if you are so selfless that you give all of yourself with the intent to fill up another person constantly, then there comes a point where you are on E (empty). Self-health includes a variety of items. It encompasses all things mental, physical, emotional, and spiritual.

Mentally: Always take time to learn something new. Plant new mental seeds and in turn your wealth of knowledge will increase. Do not let another person or thing stop you from continuing to increase your personal knowledge. Having knowledge is so powerful and it's something that once acquired no one can remove. If you don't know a word, look it up. Expand your vocabulary. Don't be afraid to speak differently. Don't be afraid to aspire to another level academically. Be the person that others aspire to be.

Emotionally: Self-doubt can tear you down, so remind yourself daily how great you are. Each morning when you wake up tell yourself I am going to accomplish something great today. Stop finding fault and find greatness. Most times we are own biggest critic. Pluck out those weeds of self-destruction as they try and sprout. Remove those around you that tear you down emotionally. Include those individuals that build you up and add to your emotional stability.

Physically: We must maintain and care for our bodies. We want to create a lifestyle that promotes good health. If we do not take the time to maintain ourselves physically, then we may not like what we see in the mirror. So, if you are able to get out there and MOVE, then MOVE. Increasing your daily physical activity will, in turn, increase your overall self-health.

Spiritually: By the second, minute, hour, and by the day, continue to water and refresh your soul. Spiritual food is needed to maintain a well-balanced life. Despite the religion, having faith in something higher than you brings a sense of assuredness and a sense of calmness that cannot be duplicated from any other source. Being sound spiritually will help to guide you in the choices you make concerning yourself and those around you.

My Self-Wealth

As I am still a work in progress, this lesson of mental, emotional, physical, and spiritual self-wealth is one for me that is ongoing. Daily on an emotional level, I try to maintain my center. Physically, my goal is to work out weekly, and an even bigger goal is to eat healthier and cleaner. Mentally, I have made sure to increase my self-knowledge by continuing my education beyond high school. I continue to try and learn something new each day and to spread that knowledge. Once someone told me, "Every time we talk, you teach me a new word." Words inspire. It's great when you can impact others. Spiritually, I personally grow closer to GOD each day and walk in accordance with his path. Increasing one's self-wealth should never stop.

Your Journal Entry of Inspiration:

How do you stay healthy; mentally, emotionally, physically and spiritually?

Toraya had her own type and her beauty was like no other.

What is the most beautiful part of you?

_____

_____

_____

Lesson 4
Beauty without Exception

Is beauty in the eye of the beholder? Well, yeah because when you look at someone and find them beautiful, the next person may look at that same person and not see beauty. We all have a unique definition of beauty.

What makes someone beautiful or handsome?

Is beauty about the shape of a person's body, the complexion of their skin, how smart a person is or is it about the clothes they wear? Beauty is a combination of all these things and more. Society and social media have a major impact on how many determine what is beautiful.

When you constantly see the same type of people or images depicted and praised as being beautiful on your television screen, in magazines, in the music videos or on social media, then you begin to form the same opinion. However, no matter how hard society tries to force a specific type of beauty on you, you must realize that beauty is YOU. We were made distinctly different for a reason, and in those differences, we should embrace each other's uniqueness. Appreciate another person's beauty for just that beauty. Do not make exceptions to beauty.

Have you ever heard someone say, "She's pretty to be a dark-skinned girl, or she's a big girl, but she's pretty, or he's cute to be a short guy?"

It's like someone could be a 10 except blah, blah. So, the next time you see someone, and you find them beautiful for whatever reason, celebrate the beauty in the person. Remove the exceptions to their beauty out of your mind and out of your conversations, and you will be amazed at how you can make another person feel.

My Beauty

As a teenager, I didn't quite know how to come to grips that my hips were wide and my thighs were fat; my feet were big, and I wasn't considered the prettiest. So, I clung to the company that made me feel I was beautiful when I didn't know or understand my self-worth.

As I grew older, I realized that these hips were on point. My feet were just that - my feet, and guess what, all of me was how GOD created me, and HE does not make mistakes.

As I grew to know my worth, I realized that beauty is me. There are so many different versions of beauty, so who is to really determine who's the prettiest and who's not? I am beautifully made. I am beautifully made, and of course, there are things about me that I work on daily, but I am determined to not overly obsess and compare my beauty or let society define it. In the end, I can only be me.

Your Journal Entry of Inspiration:

What is beautiful about you?
What makes someone beautiful or handsome?

_____

_____

_____

_____

_____

_____

_____

_____

_____

_____

_____

_____

Toraya never allowed an inability to dim the light of her abilities.

Would you ever let a negative opinion hold you back from who you want to become?

Yes or No?

_____

_____

_____

Life Lesson 5
Become "Crutchless"

Have you ever known someone that uses their past as the basis or foundation for their present? Have you yourself ever said you were a "certain way" because of what you have been through? Using what you have been through to create something great is an amazing process, but sometimes the things that happen in our past define our present in a way that causes much more harm than good. In life, use your past as a way to create a mind-boggling future. Become 'crutchless" and do not let your past handicap your future. For example, if you were abused as a child, become an advocate for the abused, not become an abuser. Duplicating behaviors happen all the time because of our past.

Become "Crutchless"

If your parents didn't graduate from high school or college, what does that mean for you?
You should go further and beyond what your parents were able to accomplish.

Become "Crutchless"

If you were constantly told that you wouldn't amount to anything because you couldn't keep your focus in school or you have a behavior issue, don't let someone else's opinion cause you to act out and to be that very thing.

Become "crutchless".

Whatever challenges you have in life, use those challenges as a platform to stand on that enables you to be "crutchless" and to walk tall and proud in the amazement that is you.

I Threw My Crutches out of the Window

My dad once said to me, "I've done some bad things in my life, and most likely you will pay for my mistakes." Hearing this at a young age made me constantly wait for failure. Failure was expected. My parents never really advocated for higher education. So honestly, as I went through my high school years, I never really aspired to be anything.

At some point, I knew I wanted to write, but I didn't know anybody around me that was a writer and successful at it. I'm pretty sure if my 18-year-old-self told someone that I wanted to be a writer, they would laugh and say, "How are you going to make a living off of writing?"

Despite all, there came a point in my life where I threw the crutches out of the window. I decided that no matter what anyone thought I could do, I knew that anything was possible. I decided that GOD had divine intervention over my life and I was not the bearer of another person's wrongdoings. I became "crutchless" and so can you.

Your Journal Entry of Inspiration:

Despite your past or current situation, what's your plan to reach your goals and to become "crutchless"?

_____

_____

_____

_____

_____

_____

_____

_____

_____

_____

_____

_____

_____

*Toraya was determined
to be great.*

*Toraya was determined
to be great.*

If you quickly reflect on where you are in life, on a scale from 1-10, how great are you?

_____

_____

_____

Share and Be an Inspiration
Post who inspires you with the hashtag
#torayawithlove

FB:
https://facebook.com/groups/torayawithlove

IG:
@focusedink

or submit via Author's site
www.focusedink.com/reviews

Life Lesson 6
Standing in Your Greatness

To stand in your greatness is a beautiful thing. There are many reasons why this may at times seem unattainable. As mentioned earlier, self-doubt can ruin your ability to stand in your greatness. Even family, friends, and associates can block your ability to stand in your greatness; standing in your greatness starts with the belief in self and belief in your ability to be great. The opportunity for greatness is in front of each one of us but navigating yourself through the struggles and obstacles that allow you to reach your goals is what divides the pack. So how do you separate yourself from the pack?

1. Be determined to be great, even when you doubt yourself or if others doubt you, your determined spirit must prevail.

Self-doubt finds a way to creep into our minds and spirits. It happens so often that we begin to believe that we can't achieve greatness. Whether it is greatness academically, in our relationships, or in achieving our personal goals, you must create an armor of determination that allows you to break through any and all barriers.

1. When presented with roadblocks, incorporate alternative routes to achieving your goals.

In life, what we plan doesn't always work out in the order as planned. However, when something stands in the way of our greatness and the goals you are trying to achieve, you must recreate the plan. You shouldn't feel discouraged. You should make adjustments and alterations to the original plan to accommodate for the obstacle ahead.

1. When life struggles present themselves, pray about it and consult emotional guidance from those who experienced similar struggles.

At times although we strive for greatness emotionally, it's all just too much. However, there is always usually a struggle on the road to greatness. So, use the tools you have within you and from loved ones to help guide you on your way.

My Greatness

Throughout the years, standing in my greatness has been uncomfortable. I tend to not share my achievements with others in fear that it will appear as if I am bragging about what I have accomplished. I dim down my light at times to not outshine others. Once, someone said to me, "I am so proud of you; you just don't know what it means to see someone that looks like me in the position that you are in."

Even when being told that I'm great, I still feel unworthy of the position at times, and I don't know whether it's deep rooted in my ancestry or because I wasn't told I was great enough as a child. I don't know. However, the older I get, I realize that I should be excited and proud about those things that I have achieved.

I am the first person in my immediate family to graduate from college and not only did I graduate I was in the top 7 of my class.

I am the first person in my immediate family to graduate from grad school.

I am the first Black woman to manage the department at its location.

I stand in my greatness, and I am proud.

1. Be determined to be great, even when you doubt your-self or if others doubt you. You're determined spirit must prevail.

2. When presented with roadblocks, incorporate alternate routes to achieving your goals.

3. When life struggles present themselves, pray about it and consult emotional guidance from those who experienced similar struggles.

Your Journal Entry of Inspiration:

What makes you great?

If you don't feel great about yourself, what are the steps needed to get you on the road to being the greatest version of you?

_____

_____

_____

_____

_____

_____

_____

_____

_____

_____

_____

_____

Toraya was determined to be the best version of Toraya.

What are you an expert at?

_____

_____

_____

Life Lesson 7
The Expert in You

What would it take to put on display the expert in you? Sometimes our shining features are not formed from what we learn out of a book but found within. Outside of your academic know how you may have some other attribute that you want to share with the world. We are all born with innate abilities. Some of us are just naturally great at a sport or have the ability to sing.

Meanwhile, some of us have to try and try hard to improve upon a skill that doesn't come naturally to us. When you know that you have truly tried to become great at a particular skill and it appears you aren't getting any better, then you may need to refocus your attention. For example, if you are not the best soccer player but you love and know the sport, there is nothing wrong with finding a way that you can still participate in the sport without actually being in the game. Supporting the team by becoming the Manager of the team may serve your need for the love of the game.

Another example would be if you can't physically perform a dance such as great dancer would but the movement of dance is in your mind and heart, then maybe you should choreograph dance or if you have a love for theater, and you can't overcome your fear of the stage, look into being behind the scenes. You don't always have to be front and center of a particular event to be a part of the reason of it being successful. There are many ways to showcase the expert in you. The expert in you can come in many shapes and forms. Rather you are the star quarterback or the water boy; it takes a team to create the win.

My Expert

Deep down in my heart, I can sing and even further down in my soul I can dance with the best of any professional. However, public opinion is still out. Despite the naysayers, I truly support the Arts. In the past, to feed my need to dance, I have tried a couple of dance classes alone, and with friends, but to no avail. My body still moves like a non-professional dancer. However, at every turn, I make it my business to attend or watch a showcase of the very thing that I love to do. I live vicariously through those who can. In the meantime, I will continue to share my expertise with those who can appreciate it.

Your Journal Entry of Inspiration:

**Even if only you believe it to be true;
What are you an expert at?
What are some activities that you love but may
not be an expert at? What can you do to
participate?**

_____

_____

_____

_____

_____

_____

_____

_____

_____

_____

_____

_____

Toraya was focused on
the prize.

Do you consider yourself as a prize? Yes or No.

_____

_____

_____

Share and Be an Inspiration
Post who inspires you with the hashtag
#torayawithlove

FB:
https://facebook.com/groups/torayawithlove

IG:
@focusedink

or submit via Author's site
www.focusedink.com/reviews

Life Lesson 8
Take Sex Out of the Driver Seat

When it comes to your body and your mind, you must consider yourself a prize. You as a prize are priceless, and your future is an even bigger prize in the making, and it too should be nurtured and safeguarded. Do not let sex cloud your vision as you journey on your path to an amazing future.

Sex is a driving force behind so many things. Some may argue that it is the driving force behind all things. Whatever the case, do not allow your imperfect nature and the need for sex to cloud your vision of yourself and your future plans. When you remove sex from the equation, things become clearer, and consequently we make better decisions. However, let's just focus on the consequences of having sex. The facts are the results could be pregnancy, sexually transmitted diseases, and a host of complicated emotions.

When you become emotionally complicated, your mental ability to focus on what's important in life can dwindle. If your true focus is to be focused on your future, then you have to remain steadfast on things that catapult you to where you want to be not causing you to remain where you are. So, always take time to clear your mind and space, and fill your mind and thoughts with how to be a better you, and if someone tries to take you off the journey to becoming a better you, you should question their motives. True friendship and true love wait for all things including sex.

My Sex Talk Made Simple.

When I was a teenager, if I had considered myself as a prize and listened to the pleas of those who said YOU SHOULD WAIT, I could have avoided multiple misjudgments and errors in life.

Your Journal Entry of Inspiration:

How will you focus on the prize? What steps will you take to make sure your judgments and future plans are set on the right path?

_____

_____

_____

_____

_____

_____

_____

_____

_____

_____

_____

_____

Toraya used the mistakes of others to learn what not to do.

If a mistake is repeated, would you still consider it a mistake? Yes or No.

_____

_____

_____

Life Lesson 9
Mistakes Happen

The mistake happens and it's just that – a mistake, and it does not happen again. However, in reality in the imperfect world which we live in; often times what we call a mistake is repeated. So, if you make the same mistake twice, is it really a mistake? Or is it intentional?

Often times we put the label of mistake on an action, when really at the moment that the action took place; we knew exactly what we were doing. However, when we look back at our labeled mistake, and we don't like what we have done, we are ashamed, and so we call it a mistake especially when we have to explain that action to others. Do not be afraid to make mistakes. The fear should become present when you don't learn from your mistakes. Beware to not use your mistakes as stumbling blocks that send you down a path that causes you to make the same mistakes repeatedly. Instead, use your mistakes as stepping stones to becoming a better version of you.

One of My Many Mistakes

Throughout the years, I have made the mistake of not forgiving. I have held grudges for years. I have done this with family members and friends. The mistake was mine because in each scenario I didn't reflect on how I was wrong in the situation. I was too busy harping on what the other person did to me. I was so blinded by their actions that I could not see my own.

However, as I grew older and lived life, I have learned the power of forgiveness, and it's a beautiful thing. Forgiveness takes a weight off you that releases you from the bondage of holding on to something that once released, you become free.

Your Journal Entry of Inspiration:

What are some mistakes you have made? What have you done or what will you do in the future to ensure you don't repeat the same mistakes?

_____

_____

_____

_____

_____

_____

_____

_____

_____

_____

_____

Toraya maintained true friendships.

Who in your life do you consider a true friend?

_____

_____

_____

Share and Be an Inspiration
Post who inspires you with the hashtag
#torayawithlove

FB:
https://facebook.com/groups/torayawithlove

IG:
@focusedink

or submit via Author's site
www.focusedink.com/reviews

Life Lesson 10
The Give and Take of Friendship

Friendship is a give and take relationship. True and meaningful friendship should be an equal divide of give and take. Always keep in mind that at various points in the relationship, one friend may give or take more than the other during times of need. However, as a friend, you have to recognize and acknowledge when it is your time to simply listen, give that truthful opinion, offer needed advice or to just be there as a shoulder to lean on.

Being able to recognize and acknowledge the needs of another individual takes time, and as a relationship grows, your instincts become keen. Throughout the years, friends will come and go, and this is normal because relationships have seasons. As an individual, you will constantly grow and change. As you grow and change, the relationships that were once amazing parts of your life become stale, lost, and even toxic. It is okay to lose a friend.

Sometimes losing a friend is losing a part of you that is no longer viable. Just think if you had a body part that begins to gangrene, you would have no choice but to cut it off because leaving it attached would cause major harm. Friendships can be similar to this. Take time out and evaluate the friendships in your life. Is the relationship causing more harm than good? Is the friendship you offer someone causing your positive vibes to be drained? If the answer is YES to either question; reevaluate. To reevaluate does not mean to get rid of a valued friendship completely.

During your reevaluation process, ask yourself a couple of questions.

1. Is this a point in the friendship where my friend needs me to just listen?
2. Is my friend going through a period in their life where they need that shoulder to lean on?

If the answer is YES, then it is perfectly reasonable to take on a burden of weight within the friendship. Sometimes it's our duty as a friend to go through life struggles with our true and close friends, together.

Here are some other questions to ask your-self during the reevaluation process.

1. Is my friend the reasons for the negative drama in their life?
2. Has my friend taken the appropriate steps within a reasonable timeframe to remove or alleviate the negativity from his or her life?

If the answer is NO, then it is okay to restructure the friendship. To restructure is to change the current level of access and energy you give the relationship. This can be as little as saying to your friend, "I'm your friend but as your friend, if you are not going to do what it takes to effect change, then I can't be involved with that particular part of your life. In extreme circumstances, sometimes the restructuring means to end the relationship totally. Be careful and choose your friends wisely. Make sure the relationships you create through life produce positive vibes more than negative harm.

A Personal Breakdown in Friendship

I had an amazing friendship with a wonderful person for years. We talked, we laughed, and we cried. I listened to her life struggles, and she listened to mine. Once we had a misunderstanding about something that I honestly can't recall all the details, but the end results were not good. Looking back on the situation, I was going through a bumpy time in my life and unbeknown to me so was she.

However, neither of us took the time to find out the root cause of our feelings, and our relationship actually hit a point where reevaluation was needed. At the time, I didn't possess the tools to evaluate our friendship properly, and therefore, I did not listen to her, and in my opinion at the time she did not listen to me in the heat of the argument, and the result was we stopped talking for years. I could have asked myself, *was the relationship causing more harm than good?* The answer would have been no.

Our relationship was not causing me harm, and in turn, I could have attempted to reevaluate our friendship, but in the heat of the argument, all I could see was what was in front of me. I didn't take the time to see potentially what could have been going on from her point of view. Fortunately, our relationship has resumed but in a different way and we have lost years in between. However, I continue to look forward at the positive in just being able to learn from our breakdown in friendship.

Your Journal Entry of Inspiration:

Are there any relationships that may need to reevaluate? If so what's your plan?

_____

_____

_____

_____

_____

_____

_____

_____

_____

_____

_____

_____

_____

Toraya lived by and displayed high standards.

Do you place high standards on yourself?
Yes or No.

_____

_____

_____

Life Lesson 11
Have Standards of Royalty

As discussed in previous lessons, to attain perfection is impossible. However, walk with the standards of royalty. Trying to reach high expectations can prove difficult at times. Yet, standards are important to keep. First, are the standards we make for our-selves. You must set standards in your life that constantly guide you in the choices and decisions you make in life. This is important because you before anyone else has to live with the choices you make. Chances are if you set high standards for yourself then this will reflect well in your decision making and result in you feeling great about yourself and others looking on in admiration.

Second, are the standards others set for you; most time this is done by your parents, family or friends. When loved ones set extremely high standards for you, this can sometimes seem unattainable. However, view the extreme standards that others set for you not as something impossible to reach but as motivation as you strive for excellence. In life, a little motivation does not hurt one bit. Be motivated and pushed by the high standards of yourself and others. Be proud to know that the standards you set for yourself will not be lowered for or by anyone. Walk with the standards of royalty.

Simply Put Standards

I noticed when I set higher standards for myself; I begin not to allow myself to make silly decisions similar to those I had made in the past. I begin to value who I was, and in turn, it reflected in the life choices I made.

Your Journal Entry of Inspiration:

What are some standards that you have set for yourself? What are some standards that others have set for you?

_____

_____

_____

_____

_____

_____

_____

_____

_____

_____

_____

_____

_____

Toraya knew the importance of reaching for her dreams.

How important is it for you to reach your
dreams or your ultimate life goals?
Very Important, Important, Not That Important
or Not Important at All
Choose One.

_____

_____

_____

Life Lesson 12
Don't Compromise You at the Expense of YOU

To compromise is to accept standards or accept expectations that are lower than what you find desirable. So, why would anyone ever compromise themselves? We all tend to find ourselves in situations where we lower the standards of ourselves or expectations of others at our own expense. As mentioned earlier, if you don't take care of you then you can be of no help to the next person. It's an amazing gift to be able to give and nurture others, but if you fall short because you neglect yourself, then the lifespan of your giving and nurturing spirit may be shortened.

You must take the steps to achieve your dreams. Achieving your dreams will help to energize and uplift you and those around you. If you don't take the time to make yourself whole, then as life passes you by you look back on pieces of your life with regret. Walk through life knowing that you reached for all the stars you wanted to reach for and that you conquered all the challenges that faced you. Don't walk through life with regret.

Don't let relationships with your mate, boyfriend, girlfriend, friends or family stop you from taking care of the needs of yourself. Sometimes we are so focused on another individual that we put our own needs on the back burner. If you place a relationship you have with another person over the relationship you have with yourself, the results are detrimental. Even if it takes you a little longer than you expected to complete a particular goal, in the end, no matter the age you still accomplished what you set out to do.

Don't compromise. Reach for the stars to become one.

My Compromise

I will say I definitely try to always take moments out for me. Me time is essential. However, there are still some moments that I have compromised my thoughts, feelings, wants, and desires. Nevertheless, I have decided that I will not let anyone stop me from seeing the sights I want to see or being in the places I want to be.

Your Journal Entry of Inspiration:

What are some of your dreams and aspirations that you will not compromise?

_____

_____

_____

_____

_____

_____

_____

_____

_____

_____

_____

_____

_____

_____

Toraya was taught to maintain a positive image on social media.

On a scale from 1-10 how important is social media to you?

_____

_____

_____

Share and Be an Inspiration
Post who inspires you with the hashtag
#torayawithlove

FB:
https://facebook.com/groups/torayawithlove

IG:
@focusedink

or submit via Author's site
www.focusedink.com/reviews

Life Lesson 13
On Social Media: What Version of You are you Selling?

These days' social media is one of the main channels of communication especially for teens and young adults. It's a platform used to stay connected with friends and family. Also, it's a platform that many use to sell and market products. You must beware not to sell the wrong version of you while posting images and videos on social media. I know some people actually want to make a spectacle out of themselves because they feel this is the way to get noticed. The thought process is, the more of a spectacle that you make out of yourself, the more likely someone will re-tweet, repost, like or share your image.

However, how do you really want to be viewed in the public eye? Be cautious before you add images to the world-wide web that you cannot take back. Since the beginning of time, we all have done things in the past that we are not proud of, the difference now is that everything is captured in a picture or in a video that can surface and resurface at different times in your life when you may want to be viewed in a different light than when the image was captured.

The fact is that many of us grow up and into responsible adults. People change. The person you are at 16 is not the person you will be at 21. The person you are at 21 is not the person you will be at 35. Therefore, start early with capturing images that you want to represent you for a lifetime. Lifetime images should be timeless. Lifetime images should reflect feelings and moments in your life that you will not be ashamed to say, "Wow, those were some amazing times." Lifetime images should be ones that when you go for a job interview, run for political office, or have a family of your own you will be able to proudly say, "Yeah that was me from back in the day." If you start to carry yourself in a way that screams, "The 'Me' now is amazing, but my future self will blow your mind," then your steps will be ordered in a way that leads you to a path of great potential.

What's My Social Status?

At one point, I was totally against social media. Then a family member encouraged me to connect via social media so that I could view pictures of my distant family and stay connected. So, I ended up starting up an account where I could share my pictures, and I could view my distant family.

Once I joined the social media craze, I loved it. It's a way to connect and share instantly. I will admit at times too much social media wreaks havoc on my soul. Therefore, as time has gone on since I first opened an account, I just log on as I have things or events to share because too much social media tends to drive me insane. However, I advocate for social media as a platform to share, but I fully understand the dangers that come along with it. Therefore, I do streamline what I post and recommend this for others as well.

Your Journal Entry of Inspiration:
What is your social media image?

_____

_____

_____

_____

_____

_____

_____

_____

_____

_____

_____

_____

_____

_____

Toraya was simply the best.

Do you consider yourself a follower or a leader?

_____

_____

_____

Life Lesson 14
Emulate Only the Best
Inspire the Rest

Befriend the best. Associate and hang out with those that have big dreams just like you. Communicate with others that have conversations that go somewhere. Join the crowd that's coming up with ideas and inventions that will change their environment, their neighborhoods, their cities, and the world. Do not become intimidated because you are not the smartest person in your circle. You always want to surround yourself with people you can learn from. You want to be among the best.

How to define the best?

1. The best are LEADERS.

2. The best are not bringing others down; they are figuring out ways to lift people up.

3. The best may not have the fanciest of clothes or things, but they have hearts of GOLD.

4. The best are always plotting their next move towards success.

5. The best are usually those that you could find strange, but if you take the time to get to know them, you will love them.

The best could be you!

My Personal Best

It has made me feel really good when people have said to me that I have inspired them to finish college because until recently I have never considered myself to be a leader. I was more of the shrink in the corner and watch what's going on around me kind of girl; 'A true introvert.' However, as I grow older and work on the best version of me, I am determined to not hide in the background any longer.

1. I am a LEADER.

2. Always plotting my next move.

3. I am on a mission to see the good in people and meet them where they are in life versus finding fault.

4. I am working on improving my heart of gold status every day.

Your Journal Entry of Inspiration:

What about your social group pushes you to be the best? What about you; makes others want to follow you?

_____

_____

_____

_____

_____

_____

_____

_____

_____

_____

_____

_____

_____

Toraya had the spirit of giving.

How important is helping those in need?
Very Important, Important, Not That Important
or Not Important at All
Choose One.

_____

_____

_____

Share and Be an Inspiration
Post who inspires you with the hashtag
#torayawithlove

FB:
https://facebook.com/groups/torayawithlove

IG:
@focusedink

or submit via Author's site
www.focusedink.com/reviews

Life Lesson 15
Be Great When No One Else is Watching

Recognition is something we all want from time to time. We want to be recognized for our accomplishments and our achievements. When we do a good deed, most times, we want it to be known that we did a great thing for someone. However, consider being great when no one else is watching. Do something amazing for someone in need just because. Being there for others and doing great deeds should become a part of who you are.

If you are always thinking of how you can help another person, you will ultimately be known for just that without even trying. After Toraya passed away, I found out several things she had done for others in need. While she was alive, her parents were not even aware of some of the selfless things Toraya did for those in need because she possessed the spirit of being great despite someone watching. It wasn't until after her death that her many acts of kindness would come to light. This is why her legacy is so great, and this is why she will always be remembered.

My Silence Awakened

Knowing and supporting Toraya for many years when no one was watching; I created this book in silence, and I didn't tell many about what I was creating because the expectation of greatness was just too high. I knew I wanted to utilize this moment in time when I was inspired by Toraya to finally begin my journey as a writer.

In the same moment, I wanted a way to continue to share Toraya's story. Toraya's parents started a foundation in her honor based in love. This book was my small way of honoring her as well.

Your Journal Entry of Inspiration:

What will you give of yourself to help others?
How can you be more selfless?

_____

_____

_____

_____

_____

_____

_____

_____

_____

_____

_____

_____

_____

_____

Toraya lived.

Fill in the blank.

Life is

_____

_____

_____

Life Lesson 16
Just Live Life

We all know the saying that life is short. So, just live it.

- -Live your dreams.
- -Live knowing that you can, and you will do amazing things even when others tell you it's impossible.
- -Live with leadership tendencies.
- Live knowing that you will not follow but that you, will be a leader that others want to follow.
- -Live to learn.
- Live knowing that through education all things, are possible.
- -Live with a higher power.
- Live knowing that there is a reason you are here and through a divine power life has been made possible.
- -Live to not shame one another.
- Live knowing that we are all different and it's those differences that make life beautiful.
- -Live with integrity.
- -Live knowing and walking in the belief that you; will be something great because if you live long enough to reflect on your life, trust me you want to be proud of YOU.
- -Live with a purpose.
- -Live knowing and constantly creating, and recreating goals that ultimately create the best version of you.
- -Live with passion.
- Live knowing who you are, what fuels you to be happy and refuel you each and every day.
- -Live with YOU.
- -Live knowing that you have to live and sit in

all the decisions and choices you make.

- -Live with the fact that tomorrow is not promised. Live knowing that there are many who no longer have breathe in their bodies to make the difference and impact in this world that you can.

So, take this journal and use it as a tool to teach others and to continuously re-teach yourself on how important life choices are and to remain grateful for the life you lead.

Your Journal Entry of Inspiration:

**What journey will you start today? What dreams
will you accomplish that you thought were
impossible?**

_____

_____

_____

_____

_____

_____

_____

_____

_____

_____

_____

_____

_____

To Raya
Sincerely, Windi

It took an eleven-year relationship that was not supposed to last and the death of Toraya for me to live my life as it was meant to be lived. I was meant to write this book, and I was meant to share my life lessons with you. So, this is only the beginning for me, and I hope this book sparks a new beginning in you to reach for those dreams that you thought were impossible to reach.

Your Journal Entry of Inspiration:
Your final thoughts

_____

_____

_____

_____

_____

_____

_____

_____

_____

_____

_____

_____

_____

Acknowledgements

I would like to acknowledge GOD first because through HIM all things are possible.

Next, I would like to thank Michael, my husband who has through all things remained at my side and motivated me to know and believe that I am Winner and that I am the Best of the Best. Thank you to Micah, my son, you are only three but you are my reason for so many things! Thank you to Macail, my daughter/the actor/the singer; you inspire me to live my dreams as you are destined for yours.

Thanks, goes out to my siblings Vernon, who is basically a one man, working machine and who shows each and every day that your hands are all you need to make a way in life and to bowl a 300! Dawn who shows and represents the spirit of I am more than what you see, I am more that you can ever imagine me to be. I am above your stereotype.

Yolanda who is determined for all things great beyond even what her eyes can see. Robert for being the responsible recipient of all the good things that come from mistakes made of those who came before him and for being a motivation to us all that if we plan a little better, our possibilities are endless. Also, to his wife Patricia for being the woman that he needed to be the man that he is. Last, Jasper whom I've had an instant friendship with since the day we met. He is an amazing example of being proud and how to never let another person dim your light.

I would like to thank my parents for coming together and bringing me into this world. My dad for introducing me to the Jazz Greats and giving me some of the most memorable summers of my life and

To my mom no words are enough to describe the immense thanks I offer to you for the sacrifices you have made. Also, thank you Denise, my other mother, for being a shining example of grace. You are always there both Michael and I.

Special thanks to all my family and friends who have supported me in all my efforts and endeavors.

I would like to especially thank John and Nicole Garvin for allowing me to get to know Toraya and for sharing her everyday JOYS from 2005 until the day she left this earth.

Thank you Toraya, you have forever changed me.

About the Author

Windi Floyd Reynolds, with roots in Georgia and Florida has a passion to write and hopes to inspire her readers to become the best version of themselves. Reynolds is a two-time graduate of Savannah State University. Reynolds, also a small business owner, entrepreneurial spirit began in 2014. She is the owner of Focused Ink Group LLC. Focused Ink Group LLC is creativity, ability and sustainability all wrapped up in one company. Windi Floyd Reynolds is an author whose creative genes simmered for years but are finally ready to be served.

Education:
B.A Mass Communications (Public Relations) minor in Business
M.S Urban Studies and Planning

Boards/Affiliations:
City of Savannah Traffic Calming Committee (2015)
Frank Callen Boys and Girls Club Sub Planning- Committee (2016)

Please visit www.focusedink.com for more information, the latest products and to sign up for The Focused Ink Blot, Reynolds' blog.

F(ink)CUSED

www.ingramcontent.com/pod-product-compliance
Lightning Source LLC
Chambersburg PA
CBHW071816090426
42737CB00012B/2111